How to
Shit Money
to Get an
iPhone

By

Dottie Randazzo

Also printed under the title "How to Shit Money!"

How to Shit Money
to Get an iPhone
by
Dottie Randazzo

Published by:

Creative Dreaming

6433 Topanga Cyn. Blvd.

Woodland Hills, CA 91303

ISBN 978-0-6152-3631-5

By Dottie Randazzo

Praying 101 for Spiritual Enlightenment
Praying 101 for Men
Praying 101 for Women
Praying 101 for Kids & Teens
Praying 101 for Parents

The Feeling
Trust
Are you a Spiritual Hypochondriac?
Gardening at Night
When the Soul Cries
How to Escape an Abusive Relationship
How to Shit Money!

Fiction
The Blue Girl

Frugality is founded on
the principal that all
riches have limits. –
Edmund Burke

Introduction

If you are here reading this, then kudos to you. You actually got past the title of this book.

I want to take a moment to talk about the word "shit." While I realize it does not necessarily have a positive connotation, I have used it because it is something that is a normal part of life. Hence, money should be as much a normal part of your life as a shit is.

Since I am here and since I can, I will share with you some interesting information I found in the Etymology Dictionary. For those of you who aren't familiar with the word etymology, it means origin of a word.

It is rumored, but impossible to prove, that the word shit is an acronym that was used in the shipping industry for "ship high in transit," which meant "don't store below deck" since, in the 17th century, everything under the sun was being shipped to all corners of the globe. However, shit is not an acronym. The word itself is, in fact a good 1,000 years older than the common use of acronyms. And if you want to get technical, the verb is the original form; the noun derives from it.

Dictionary.com indicates the word "shit" means: excrements, feces, an act of defecating, evacuation. It is also a slang for pretense, lies, exaggeration, non-sense, something inferior or worth-less, selfish, mean or otherwise contemptible person; narcotic drugs, possessions, equipment, mementos, etc., stuff.

But here in this book, "shit" is used as a metaphor, a figure of speech in which a term or phrase is applied to something, but to which it is not literally applicable, in order to suggest a resemblance. Hence, you want to be able to have money coming into your life as often as you shit!

OK, so learning about shit is not why you bought this book, is it?

Let's talk about the word "money." Do you know how many different words can be associated with money? Here are a few: mint, pecuniary, monetary, cash, take, cashier, account, handicap, fee, mazuma, impecunious, purse, spend, meritorious, specie, fine, sterling, sock, moolah, expense, miser, post, prostitute, stock, wallet, interest, greenback, teller, yield, flush, outlay, smacker, con, overcharge, underwrite, bail, currency, gratuity, tip, pouch, pay, satchel, pony, subsidy, indebted, fiscal, cent, coin, subscribe, riches, policy, assets, income, squander, receipt, kitty, collect, inflation, invest, dough, principal, exempt, bill, mark, fund, afford, blackmail, kite, laundry, grease, run, refund, profit, advance, tuition, nut greedy, finance, and pocket. Get the picture? I am sure there are a few I have not listed.

The point is, these words are associated with money every single day, probably on more than one occasion. They are used as often as you shit.

You cannot fix what you cannot identify. This is a phrase that will be repeated in this book. The purpose is to get you back on track so that you can see why you aren't shitting money now.

These questions and exercises can't be done in an hour or even a week. They require a lot of thought in your spare time.

The way you *feel* about money and the way you treat it are in accordance with beliefs that you formed when you were a child.

If one of your first experiences regarding money was to watch your parents fight over it, chances are you attach a degree of conflict to money.

Your gender also affects how you perceived money as a child.

In my instance, my Mom was a homemaker and my Dad brought home the money. Seeing this as a small child, I vowed I would never put myself in my mother's position to have to ask anyone for money.

Did you hear
stereotype messages
growing up regarding
money?

Was it something like,
"Men are supposed to
be the bread winners"?

What relationship
messages did you hear
about money?

Does this sound familiar? "It is just as easy to fall in love with a rich man as a poor man."

As a boy, you may have associated money with power. In some situations, it is the person with the money who controls a relationship and is the decision maker.

To men, money can represent identity and power.

To women, money can represent security and autonomy.

Some women end up
with low self-esteem
due to their lack of
information and
control over their
money.

Indeed, men and women have different money styles. Your money style often comes from your parents.

A tightwad parent may have told you that people who spend money are irresponsible people.

Economic conditions growing up can affect a person's money style, too.

In sum, looking at your money style is a great way to examine your behavior around money. For example:

Hoarding or keeping a tight hold of money can result from distrust of others and/or fear of the future.

Those who take in, acquire, and achieve always look outside of themselves for proof that they are worthy.

For those who want to take over and control, the power means more than the money itself.

Spending addicts get the thrill from the transaction.

Messy money people are the ones who are always overdrawn at the bank and/or overcharging on their credit cards.

There are people who are
paralyzed by money.
They don't waste it and
they don't spend it. It just
sits there.

Remember, you can't fix
it if you can't identify it.

Women tend to define themselves through relationships. They see money as a way to take care of themselves and others.

In general, men are more
self-confident and self-
assured about money
than women.

Maybe your parents didn't talk about money, like they didn't talk about sex – kept it secret and hush-hush. This kind of behavior could instill a belief that money is private or that money is bad and, therefore, we just don't mention it.

Whether you heard about money or didn't, you formed opinions in your mind that control your actions today.

While growing up, was
money a source of
conflict in your family?

Were your parents
extravagant with money
or tight-fisted?

How did you feel when
you saw your parents'
interaction with money?

What is the one thing that
you learned from your
family regarding money
that you want to pass on
to your children?

What is the one thing that you learned from your family regarding money that you want to let go of?

How did you feel as a
child when you learned
that there are rich people
and poor people?

Since you are reading this
book, I think it is safe to
say you were not a rich
child discovering that
there are poor people in
the world.

Did you grow up hearing
that money was the root
of all evil?

Chances are you don't
want to be an evil person
or do evil things. And if
you think that money is
the root of all evil – well,
as you are pushing away
the evil, you are pushing
away the money.

Did you grow up hearing
the phrase "filthy rich"?

Did anyone explain to you when you were a child the differences between rich people and poor people?

Do you remember how you felt hearing this?

How did you treat your birthday money as a child?

Were you encouraged to save part or all of it?

Were you taken to the store immediately to spend it?

All of these questions will dredge up your deep-seeded thoughts regarding money to the surface. Once you see what your thoughts, beliefs and *feelings* are regarding money, you will be able to identify the areas that you need to change.

Growing up, did you have to account to your parents for every expenditure that you made?

As you got older, were
more strings attached to
the money that was given
to you, or fewer?

If you ever borrowed money from your parents, as a child or an adult, were there restrictions, explicit or hidden, as to how you could spend it?

Do you think these restrictions were reasonable?

Was money ever given to you conditionally on how well you behaved, what you accomplished, your school grades, or just to keep you out of trouble?

What money were you ever, if ever, given unconditionally with no strings attached, just because?

You can't fix what you
can't identify.

Do you think that your parents would approve of how you handle money now?

Do you think that your parents would trust you to manage a large sum of money wisely?

What were you taught about money, receiving money, making money?

What has it been like discussing money with a spouse or a lover?

Based on the questions asked so far, and the answers you have come up with, do you still have those same feelings about money today?

To create a money-filled
life, you will have to
think differently about
money.

To create a money-filled life, you will have to change your belief system about money.

To create a money-filled
life, you will have to *feel*
differently about money.

When you change, the money in your life will change.

Imagine that you are
given the task of judging
yourself today on how
you have handled money
in the past. How would
you judge yourself?

What is your reaction
toward money?

Would your reaction be different if you inherited $10,000 versus winning it in the lottery?

Would your reaction be different if you saved $10,000 versus completing a work project and receiving $10,000?

What are the ways in
which money can affect
your life positively?

What are the ways that
money can affect your
life negatively?

Your identity or self-image is what you hold to be true about yourself.

Your self-esteem is the reputation you have with yourself.

How do you view
yourself regarding
money?

What is your current belief system that you have created about money?

Do you know what it is?

Chances are no one has ever asked you this question before.

I am asking you now –
What do you believe to
be true about money?

Your belief system is the
core of your money
issues.

If you believe that in the future you will have money and then you will be set and happy, you will never have the money you desire. Hence, you will never have the happiness you have planned for the future.

The future never gets
here. The present is
always here and that is
what is important – right
here and right now.

Money does not buy happiness. Happiness is internal and money is external. The effect money will have on you internally will be as lasting as the scent of a flower. Thinking that money will bring you happiness is a great game of illusion and delusion that you are playing with yourself.

Do you value money?

Think about this for a
moment.

Would you stop what
you are doing and bend
down to pick up a penny
from the ground?

If not, why not?

A penny is money and it
has the value of a penny.

If you don't appreciate
and value a penny, will
you appreciate and value
a nickel?

A penny is of less monetary value than a nickel. However, it is still considered money.

When you learn to value a penny and be grateful that you have the opportunity to be a penny richer, the laws of attraction kick in big time. The universe feels and responds to your energy. So the universe says, "Wow, that dude or dudette values a penny and is grateful for a penny. Let's send him or her some more."

A grateful soul is a
blessed soul.

How do you treat
money?

Do you feel as if you have to spend it the minute you get it?

Do you feel that it will
burn a hole in your
pocket if you keep it too
long?

Do you hang onto every
penny as if it were the
last?

Really think about these questions.

You can't fix what you can't identify.

The only wrong answer
is the one that you think
is the right answer, but
really isn't how you *feel*
inside.

Be truthful and honest.

No one is going to judge
you.

Money is energy. It comes and goes. It is just as important to give as it is to receive. If you don't let someone give you something, you are denying that person the opportunity to give. It's a two-way street.

Think of money as a revolving door. We so freely open the door for money to come in and yet hold on to it very tightly when we have to let some of the money go. What you don't realize is that the door cannot swing outward for the money to come in freely if you are holding it so tightly in order not to let any out. Also, by holding the door tightly, you are telling God or the masters of the universe that you don't truly believe that you will be blessed abundantly; therefore, you are hanging onto every penny. Money is just like grains of sand – the more you squeeze your fist to hold the sand in, the more sand slips through your fingers.

The more you hang onto
your money, the more
opportunities to spend it
will come along – either
in the way of car repairs,
medical bills or some
other non-fun thing.

Is your identity attached
to money?

Are you what you own?

If your identity is attached to the things you own, then you aren't being the real you and chances are you don't even know who the real you is.

If your things were to disappear right now and you were asked who you are, would you be able to answer the question?

How would you feel if everything you owned and associated yourself with disappeared?

What would you miss the most?

What would you be glad
to get rid of?

How would you *feel*?

Would you be looking around for someone or something to identify you?

Come on, think about
this. This is serious stuff.

You can't fix what you
can't identify.

How do you *feel* when you have to spend money?

How do you *feel* when you pay the bill at the grocery store or restaurant?

Are you thankful for the opportunity to provide a way for another human being to feed his family, purchase medicine, or help educate and cloth his or her family?

When you spend money, do you *feel* as if something is being taken away from you?

Do you *feel* that you are
getting ripped off?

Everyone on this planet
has the right to earn a
living.

What do you think about money?

How do you think about
money?

Do you think money is only for a few and that you are not included?

Do you think that there is
a limited supply of
money on the planet?

According to Russell Schofield, quantum physics can be defined as, "Thought directs energy and energy follows thought."

Everything around you is made up of energy – tiny protons, molecules and atoms, all vibrating to create something, be it a table, chair, coin or piece of paper – money. All of these things are not just energy. They are energy that came from thought.

What are your emotional
issues with money?

Fear blocks the flow of money – just as a salesman whose existence is riding on a sale that he won't be able to make.

Hmmmmm… knowing that, don't you think it is vital that you think positive about money in your life?

Do you hoard your
money?

Are you greedy with
your money?

Do you believe in lack
and scarcity?

Do you believe you can actually live an abundant life, free of money worries?

Does this sound
impossible?

It isn't impossible. But it does require a concerted, conscious effort and hard work. Changing your mind is probably the hardest work you will ever have to do in life. The ego is stubborn and wants to hold onto the beliefs that have, up until this time, identified who you are and what you believe about yourself and money.

When you get rid of that fear and negativity that you have associated with money, it will then begin to flow into your life.

Money affects how you *feel*, think, and behave.

Appreciation accelerates
manifestation.

When you are thankful and grateful for what you have, the universe will send you more! If you are complaining about what you have or want, you are not being grateful for what is already in your life.

If all you have are two pennies, start each day with those two pennies in front of you. Be truly thankful for those two pennies. Look at them as money. They are, indeed, money.

Write down everything that you want to have or accomplish in life. Do not think about the cost. Most people think of the cost of something and that determines whether or not they can attain it. You don't walk out the door every morning with a guarantee that you will walk back in. But you do it with an expectancy and certainty that you will walk back in the door at some point in the evening.

What if you were to think about walking back into your door and money the same way?

You merely know what
you want and with
expectancy and certainty
know that in some way,
somehow, you will get it.

The hardest part is "just knowing" what you want.

Too much brain power is spent thinking about <u>how</u> money will come.

Some people spend a lot of time creating corporations to hide money that they haven't even made yet. And somehow, they know that when they make all that money, someone is going to come along and steal it. To me, that is like a squirrel digging a hole for the nut he hasn't found yet. They just don't do that. Yet, most people worry about what will happen to their fortune before they even have sight of it.

By now, you probably have a pretty good idea about how you *feel* and think about money. You should have a good idea what beliefs you have held onto about money.

Now all ya gotta do is
change your beliefs and
the money will change.

Wealth operates, just like everything else, by the basic rules of life, such as:

Your perception is your reality.

Your power is where you put your belief system.

You were born with free will.

Exercise your free will to create beliefs.

Your beliefs will be your reality.

You are the creator of your life.

You are the only one responsible for the life you choose to live.

If, for some reason, you aren't sure about any of these basic rules, you may have a few more books to read. If, on the other hand, you have filtered through all the bullshit you have been taught or told and you have wised up to understand these basic rules, you will have absolutely no problem mastering how to shit money!

Write down any fears you may have regarding money. Imagine how you are going to deal with those fears. What actions or remedies will be necessary to remove these obstacles and your fears?

Imagine the largest amount of money you can think of in front of you. I want you to become aware of how your body is reacting to this money. Notice your breathing, your pulse and your heartbeat.

What are you *feeling?*

Are you *feeling* panic?

Are you *feeling* anxiety?

Are you *feeling* scared?

Are you *feeling*
overwhelmed?

Are you *feeling* happy?

Are you *feeling* worthy?

Write these *feelings* down.

Did you know you had
these *feelings* regarding
large sums of money?

Are there individuals or groups that can help you overcome your fears or negative feelings? Who else will be able to understand what you're going through?

Take some time alone and sit and imagine yourself in a room full of money and this money is alive. Yep, it's talking money! You are going to have a conversation with this money and it's going to have a conversation with you. This is just like you did as a child when you played with your imaginary friends. Chances are there were times when you were shocked by the stuff that your imaginary friends told you. Likewise, you may be surprised what this money tells you, or by what you tell the money. Do this exercise every day until you make friends with the talking money. Sit quietly and consciously talk to this money. Force yourself to talk about how this money *feels* to you, what it represents. Make friends with it. Laugh with it. Know that money is made of the same energy that you are made of, that your friends are made of. And you want money to be your best friend. You want money to be as available to you as your friends are. You want to have as much fun with money as you do with your friends. You don't take your friends so seriously and you shouldn't take money so seriously either. Chat with it, laugh with it. Make that money feel like the perfect relation-ship feels – it's free to come and go. You love it when it's here and you love it when it's not. You aren't going to hang on to it and suffocate it. You are going to let that money know that it does not identify you. You are you and it is money. Share the wonderful stories of all the fun you will have with money. As ridiculous as this sounds, I think it would be safe to say that the mindset of most people regarding money is far more ridiculous. Some people act as if they can actually take it with them when they die. Go figure.

Another exercise for you to do is to think about what your life would have been like had you been born wealthy. What kind of schools would you have gone to? What kind of home would you have grown up in? What kind of friends would you have had? What kind of job would you have? How would you *feel* right now?

So now we come to the end and this is where you think to yourself, *"This is it?"*

Yep, that's it. It takes more time to unload baggage than it does to get off the ground and fly.

Once you have identified your beliefs, you can change them. You can believe whatever your heart desires about money. And since what you believe is what you will create, I think you should create some awesome beliefs.

Make the decision to
change your attitude and
beliefs about money.

Release any beliefs that you are discovering no longer serve you well.

How about:

"I believe that I am
worthy of shitting
money!"

"I believe that money is
energy."

"I believe that money is
abundant and fun!"

"I believe money comes to me constantly from directions I cannot even imagine." That's my personal favorite. It's like telling the universe, "Go ahead and surprise me." And it does, and it is wild!

"I believe that money is good and fun to share."

You will know that you really believe what you are saying when you can *feel* a tingly vibration on your skin. That's the energy you are sending out of yourself into the universe for your intentions to be fulfilled.

www.ingramcontent.com/pod-product-compliance
Lightning Source LLC
Chambersburg PA
CBHW020206200326
41521CB00005BA/255